What do you Do with a feeling?

Your Guide
To Becoming A Feelings Expert

By Tasha Belix & Jo-Ann Godenir

◆ FriesenPress

Suite 300 - 990 Fort St
Victoria, BC, V8V 3K2
Canada

www.friesenpress.com

Illustrations by Jo-Ann Godenir

Learning to identify and manage our emotions is an important part of getting our needs met and living a healthy life.

ISBN
978-1-5255-3536-9 (Hardcover)
978-1-5255-3537-6 (Paperback)
978-1-5255-3538-3 (eBook)

1. Juvenile Nonfiction

Distributed to the trade by The Ingram Book Company

This book is dedicated to:

_____

A gift from:

_____

Because:_____

_____

_____

Everyone has feelings

Feelings are like a map; they guide us to help navigate problems and find solutions.

Feelings are an IMPORTANT Part of us

Feelings are not **good** or **bad**, they just are.

Some feelings like happiness and being loved are easier to hold than others

It doesn't feel good when we (hide) or ignore our feelings. They usually pop up in a sore stomach, headache or bossy thoughts.

or we feel numb

Be curious about how you feel

feelings tell us we, NEED Something

Feelings are sending us messages
we need to hear. Sometimes we have a
"gut feeling,"

but we don't always have the words
to describe it. People call this feeling
" intuition."

Intuition is usually a very wise part of
us trying to be heard.

Pay-Attention to your feelings

It can feel like a *bubble*
in your throat that wants
to say something.

It can feel like tears
are trying to *escape* from
your eyes even though
you don't want them to.

It's a sinking

feeling in your heart
that makes it hard
to *breathe*.

We feel feelings in our Body

When someone **names** our feeling
it helps **tame** our feeling. A really cool
brain scientist, Dan Siegel, says:

"Name it to tame it."

This means when we name a feeling, it helps
connect the *emotional* side of our brain with
the *logical* side of our brain.

That helps us understand - *and deal
with* - feelings that seem overwhelming.
It's a right/left brain thing.

every feeling has a NAME

Like many other forces in nature,
feelings will come and go.

The sun will rise and set each day,
waves will kiss the shore
and retreat to the ocean,
breath flows in and out again,
and again, and again.

We can ride the waves of emotion better by
taking *slow, deep breaths* in for the count of
four and then out again for the count of four.

all feelings have a beginning and an end

Cheat Sheet:

What are our feelings trying to tell us?

They are expressing a **need.** Meeting the need is essential when handling emotions.

Sadness needs company, a **hug,** or loving touch.

Anger prefers validation and s p a c e - not a hug! P.S. A cuddle comes later.

Fear wants **reassurance,** protection, and safety.

heavy feelings get lighter when we share them

No one is born knowing what to do with feelings

Someone has to show us what to do with them

Humans are hardwired to **connect** with **others** from the very start of life, and it's through a relationship with another person that we *learn* to take care of our emotions.

When we are little, someone else needs to *soothe* our emotions *over and over again*. With time, we learn how to do this for ourselves.

When we know how to **take care** of our emotions, we feel better about ourselves and can make new **choices**.

What we feel is OK

When you feel like you are
"losing it," try *moving* it!

You could *do* jumping jacks,

take a walk,

shoot hoops,

draw a picture,

or *play* with your cat.

Our feelings tell us we need to DO Something

Some people feel things BIGGER than others and that is OK

P.S. these people are called SUPER-feelers

Super-feelers walk around with their "feelings dial" at high volume and need special support to learn ways to turn down this *super-feeling* power.

Without understanding, super-feelers can often feel overwhelmed and hold their feelings inside.

You might be a super-feeler if you….

Feel **big** emotions like worries, or happy, sad, scared, excited and frustrated.

Have a heart that **pounds** really hard.
Are *shy* or have a face that turns red easily.
Feel especially *sensitive* to yelling and fighting.
'Catch' feelings like they are **contagious**! When other people feel sad, a super-feeler feels sad too.

Experience **bad dreams** after you watch a scary movie or hear about something bad on the news.
Act like a mini-teacher at school, trying to manage **other people's emotions** to feel better inside.

You sort of *feel* other people's feelings.
And it doesn't always *feel* like a good thing.

We all need someone to See Us and get us

When we are
sad MAD
or scared

Validating what someone is feeling,
without judgement, can be hard to do at first.

Stopping to let them know you really "hear"
them, helps make the feeling smaller and lets
them know they are not alone.

Remember that our
body language says a lot.
Eye contact, *loving touch*, and *soft
tone of voice* are the best ways to
acknowledge a feeling.

(except for **anger**, which DOES NOT want a hug).

Cheat Sheet:

I can only imagine how _____ (feeling) you must feel, because _____, because _____, because _____.

For example:
I can only imagine how *angry* you must be, *because you are someone who really cares about things being fair*, because even though you followed the rules, your brother didn't, because he acts like he can do whatever he wants. *I can see why you'd feel so angry.*

It makes sense that you are feeling *sad, because your closest friendship has changed*, because you really trust this person and like spending time with her, because there isn't anything you can do to make her change the way she feels. *It's sad when friendships change.*

if our big people are scared of their hard feelings

they might accidentally teach us to be scared of our big feelings too!

When *actively listening* to someone's emotions, it is important to let them know you are there to support them. You can say things like

"*I hear you*"
or "*You are not alone*"

(and then just LISTEN).

feelings need SUPPORT (not solutions)

feelings are a beautiful part of us that tell us we need something if we listen to them

Even though we might *worry* that some feelings will never end, like how we feel after the loss of someone we love, they do change over time.

Sometimes we might wish a feeling would last **forever,** like how we feel when we hold our baby for the first time. Just thinking of that feeling makes **happy** tears come to our eyes, but we don't feel that every moment of every day.

no feeling lasts forever

Knowing what to do with feelings
is like having a **lantern** inside of you.

It helps **guide** you through life and
keep you **safe,** no matter the weather.

What do you do with your feelings?

About the Author:

Tasha Belix is a Registered Psychologist who has specialized in youth and families for twenty years. She has advanced training in affective neuroscience, trauma-informed care, EMDR, emotion-focused family therapy and The Juno House Model. She truly believes in the importance of moving feelings through the body. Tasha lives in Calgary, Alberta, with her husband, three kids, their cat, Licky, and dog, Pepper. *What Do You Do with a Feeling?* is the first book in a series.

About the Illustrator:

Jo-Ann Godenir is a multi-discipline artist with a passion for creating works of colour and visual delight. Self-professed super-feeler and mother of two spitfires, she has learned first-hand the importance of paying attention to and taking care of our feelings. This is her first children's book collaboration.

CPSIA information can be obtained
at www.ICGtesting.com
Printed in the USA
LVHW071148220919
R15192800001B/R151928PG631746LVX1B/1/P

9 781525 535376